Volcanoes

Disaster & Survival

Stephanie Buckwalter

Enslow Publishers, Inc.

40 Industrial Road   PO Box 38
Box 398   Aldershot
Berkeley Heights, NJ 07922   Hants GU12 6BP
USA   UK

http://www.enslow.com

Library of Congress Cataloging-in-Publication Data:

Buckwalter, Stephanie.
    Volcanoes : disaster & survival / Stephanie Buckwalter.
        p. cm. — (Deadly disasters)
    Includes bibliographical references and index.
    ISBN 0-7660-2384-2
    1. Volcanoes—Juvenile literature. I. Title. II. Series.
QE521.3.B82 2005
551.21—dc22

                        2004011928

To Our Readers: We have done our best to make sure all Internet Addresses in this book were active and appropriate when we went to press. However, the author and the publisher have no control over and assume no liability for the material available on those Internet sites or on other Web sites they may link to. Any comments or suggestions can be sent by e-mail to comments@enslow.com or to the address on the back cover.

Illustration Credits: Associated Press, AP, pp. 4, 12, 14 (first, second, fifth and sixth photos), 15, 23, 25, 26, 29, 39, 41, 42, 43 (background); Associated Press, The Daily News, p. 36; Associated Press, Mark Headrick, p. 40; Bobbie Myers, USGS, p. 9; David Hardy/Science Photo Library, pp. 21, 27; Enslow Publishers, Inc., p. 11; Library of Congress, Prints and Photographs Division, p. 18; Lyn Topinka, USGS, p. 6; Matthew Shipp/Science Photo Library, p. 14 (fourth photo down); S. Harlow, USGS, p. 1; USGS, pp. 14 (third photo and last photo), 32, 34.

Cover Illustration: S. Harlow, USGS

Contents

Mount St. Helens is part of the Cascade Mountain Range, which has many volcanoes. Mount St. Helens erupted with explosive force in 1980.

Mount St. Helens Blows Its Top

"VANCOUVER, VANCOUVER, THIS IS IT!"[1] THE LAST words of scientist David Johnston burst over the airwaves on May 18, 1980. Moments later, a wall of volcanic debris came barreling toward him.

Johnston was working at the U.S. Geological Survey observation post, just six miles from Mount St. Helens. He was a special kind of scientist who studied volcanoes, called a volcanologist. Johnston was trying to alert a base station in Vancouver, Washington. The volcano had shown signs of activity for the past two months. In fact, just an hour and a half earlier, Johnston had reported that things were "normal" on the mountain. After he had alerted Vancouver, he was killed by the blast.

At 8:32 A.M., geologists Dorothy and Keith Stoffel were flying over the summit, or top, of Mount St. Helens in a small plane. Eleven seconds later, the mountain literally blew its top, removing 1,312 feet of ice and rock. The Stoffels described what occurred next. "Within a matter of seconds, perhaps 15 seconds, the whole north side of the summit crater began to move instantaneously. . . . The nature of movement was eerie. The entire mass began to

Spirit Lake was completely changed by the eruption of Mount St. Helens.

ripple and churn up, without moving laterally. Then the entire north side of the summit began sliding . . . ."[2]

The mountain blew out to the side, shooting a wave of very hot gases and pulverized rock, called a pyroclastic flow, across the landscape. Nearest to the blast, what once was a forest was now barren land. Trees up to fourteen miles out from the volcano snapped off at their bases. They were also stripped of their leaves and branches. A few miles beyond that, trees remained standing but were scorched brown.

"Vancouver, Vancouver, this is it!"

—Scientist David Johnston, who was killed by the Mount St. Helens eruption.

Spirit Lake, north of the mountain, was instantly changed. The landslide deposited so much rock and debris in the lake that its elevation rose by almost two hundred feet. The wave of hot gases raised the surface temperature of the water from 42° to 100° Fahrenheit (6° to 38° Celsius), killing everything that lived in it. In total, fifty-seven people and an estimated twenty-four thousand animals died on Mount St. Helens that day.[3]

Volcanoes are a natural disaster that cannot be prevented. At best, they can be studied. The knowledge gained can be used to predict events and save lives.

CHAPTER 2

Volcanoes Up Close

CAN A VOLCANO RISE UP OVERNIGHT? THE ANSWER in most cases is no. However, that did happen to Dioniso and Paula Pulido. They lived in Mexico in an area surrounded by long-dead volcanoes. On the afternoon of February 20, 1943, Paula was watching their sheep with her small son. Her husband cleared branches across the field. Paula saw a small whirlwind coming toward her, with a crevice, or large crack, forming behind it. Before long, a smoking hole appeared along the crevice. Dioniso soon noticed the crevice and the hole, too.

Suddenly, they saw ashes rising above part of the crevice. Paula saw the nearby trees catch fire. She later explained, "Then the ground rose in the form of a confused cake above the open fissure, and then disappeared,

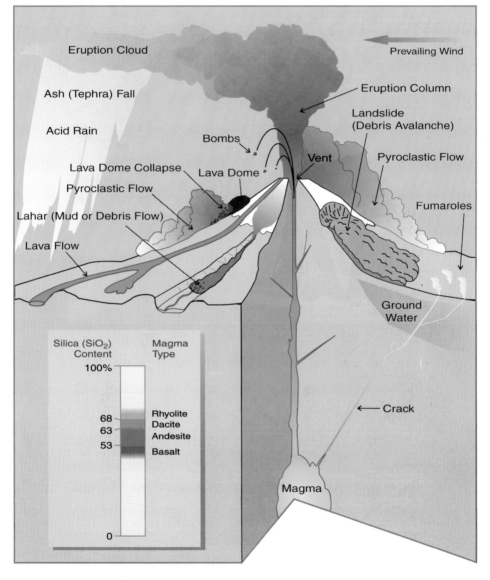

Eruption Cloud

Prevailing Wind

Ash (Tephra) Fall

Eruption Column

Acid Rain

Landslide
(Debris Avalanche)

Bombs

Vent

Pyroclastic Flow

Lava Dome Collapse

Lava Dome

Pyroclastic Flow

Fumaroles

Lahar (Mud or Debris Flow)

Lava Flow

Ground
Water

Silica (SiO$_2$)
Content

Magma
Type

100%

68 — Rhyolite
Dacite
63 — Andesite
53 — Basalt

Crack

0 —

Magma

When a volcano erupts, different kinds of dangerous substances
can come out of the mountain. These include hot steam, rock, big
globs of lava called "lava bombs," lava rivers, and toxic gases.

9

but I cannot say whether it blew out or fell back—I believe it swallowed itself. I was sure the earth was on fire."[1] By the next day, the volcano was 33 feet tall. By the end of the week, it grew to a height of 463 feet. A year later it measured 1,102 feet tall. The volcano was named Parícutin. Scientists were able to study it from the time it was "born" until it ceased activity nine years later.

How and Where Volcanoes Form

The earth's crust is made up of several huge pieces, called plates. These plates slide around slowly on a rocky layer of the earth called the ductile mantle layer. When they collide, the plate that plunges into the earth causes mantle to melt. This creates magma. Magma rises and erupts at the earth's surface. This forms volcanoes. When magma emerges from a volcano, it is called lava.

Most of the world's volcanoes are found along the edges of plates. More than half of the world's active volcanoes circle the Pacific Ocean in an area commonly called the "Ring of Fire." Other active volcanoes are found along the Mediterranean Sea (southern Europe to central Asia) and in the Hawaiian Islands, Iceland, and East Africa.

Five Types of Volcanoes

There are five basic types of volcanoes—shield, cinder cone, composite or stratovolcanoes, lava domes, and

Most volcanoes are found in the Ring of Fire.

calderas. Shield volcanoes are formed by thin, runny lava. They tend to take up a wide area and have gently sloping sides. Cinder cone volcanoes, like Parícutin, throw ash and small rocks into the air that pile up right around the vent. The sides tend to be steep, but the volcanoes are not very tall. Composite volcanoes are usually very tall with steep sides. They are formed by cycles of mild and explosive eruptions. Lava domes are often found in the craters or on the sides of large composite volcanoes. The domes are formed when small amounts of thick lava pile near its vent. Calderas are places where the earth's surface collapses to form a large hole. They form when magma erupts explosively from a shallow chamber. The largest

11

1. Caldera
2. Cinder Cone
3. Shield Volcano
4. Stratovolcano
5. Lava Dome

Each type of volcano looks and acts differently from the others.

volcanoes on earth are calderas. The Yellowstone Caldera in Yellowstone National Park is forty-five miles across.

Seven Types of Eruptions

Shield, cinder cone, lava domes, and composite volcanoes are built over time by many eruptions. Volcanologists classify eruptions by how explosive they are. Some eruptions are harmless lava flows. Others are huge explosions that devastate everything in their paths and can affect people very far away. The strength of an eruption is rated on something called the Volcano Explosivity Index (VEI). An eruption's VEI is rated from 1, the weakest, to 8, the strongest. The table on page 14 describes the various eruptions in order of least explosive to most explosive. Most are named after a volcano that was first seen erupting that way.

Volcano Monitoring

Volcanologists can forecast the likelihood of an eruption by studying a volcano. Ideally, they would have a diary of the volcano's day-to-day behavior and know the eruptive history. Unfortunately, this information is not available on many of the world's volcanoes. Instead, scientists use other methods to predict an eruption.

Scientists can test the gases coming from the volcano. When an increase in certain gases, such as hydrogen and

Types of Volcanic Eruptions

Type	Description	Reality	Examples	VEI
Hawaiian	Emits large amounts of runny lava, producing large volcanoes with gentle slopes.		Kilauea, Hawaii; Hekla, Iceland	0–1
Strombolian	Mild eruptions of small lava bombs, ash, gas, and glowing cinders that look much like fireworks. Can produce lava flows.		Stromboli, Italy; Parícutin, Mexico	1–2
Phreatic	Caused by cold ground or surface water touching hot rock or magma. Only pieces of rock erupt.		Tual Volcano, Philippines; La Soufrière, Guadeloupe	1–4
Vulcanian	Repeated explosions of fine ash and large lava bombs that are thrown far from the vent.		Vulcano, Italy; Mount Fuji, Japan	2–4
Vesuvian	Discharges of ash and gas in the shape of a cauliflower-shaped cloud.		Vesuvius, Italy	3–7
Peléan	Violent explosion directed as an avalanche to the side of the volcano. Emits thick lava with a burning cloud of ash, gases, and magma fragments.		Mt. Pelée, Martinique; Lassen Peak, California, U.S.A.	4–6
Plinian and Ultra-Plinian	Explosive eruptions that send ash, magma fragments, and cinders high into the atmosphere.		Mount St. Helens, USA; Krakatoa, Indonesia	4–8

Source: U.S. Geological Survey

sulfur dioxide is measured, the eruption is close. Those in nearby areas can then be told to leave or take other precautions.

Volcanologists also monitor ground deformation. On Mount St. Helens, the ground changed shape, bulging outward. Deformation has typically been detected by using tiltmeters and laser beams. Tiltmeters measure the slope of the earth's surface. Laser beams measure the distance between various points on the volcano. This type

Two scientists set up a Global Positioning System (GPS) device on Mount St. Helens. The device will monitor the ground for movement and transmit the data via satellite.

of equipment was available on Mount St. Helens. However, it was placed too far down on the mountain to detect the bulge growing. Volcanologists are currently experimenting with using satellites, like those of the Global Positioning System (GPS). With these, they hope to pinpoint and measure deformations.

Studying earthquakes is another way to monitor volcanoes. Earthquakes and volcanoes go hand in hand. One can trigger the other. Moving magma can cause an earthquake. As magma rises to the surface, it often has to break through rock, creating earthquakes. Many people describe feeling vibrations for days, weeks, or even months in advance of an eruption.

When the eruption actually occurs, the vibrations are a little different from those of an earthquake. Dr. J. P. van der Stok, a scientist who documented the initial eruption of Krakatoa, noted the difference. Simon Winchester, in his book on Krakatoa reports,

> The vibrations were not so much being felt through [van der Stok's] feet, as if they had emanated from somewhere deep in the earth; they were in fact being felt *in the air*. . . . most of the shaking was coming through the very atmosphere itself. And vibration of this kind was the very particular hallmark of an erupting volcano. . .[2]

Seismographs are used to measure vibrations in the ground. The widespread use of seismographs was just starting when Krakatoa erupted in the late 1800s.

CHAPTER 3

Krakatoa Makes Waves

O N AUGUST 26, 1883, THE VOLCANO NAMED Krakatoa exploded. Very little of the mountain, or the island it was on, was left behind. The volcanoes in the Dutch East Indies (now Indonesia) were frequently active in the 1800s. Rumbling and smoke were almost daily occurrences in the numerous volcanoes on the islands of Java and Sumatra. Krakatoa sat between the two islands.

The sound of the eruption was heard three thousand miles away. Throughout the world scientific equipment detected changes in the tides and air pressure. Volcanic ash in the atmosphere changed the colors of sunsets around the globe for the next few years.

The biggest impact was on the islanders. In just a few hours, 36,417 people died and 165 villages were destroyed.

However, it was not the actual volcanic eruption that did the damage, for Krakatoa was uninhabited at that time. A volcano near the sea can cause great ocean waves, called tsunamis. These devastated the islands. Krakatoa was a volcano that no one would forget.

Krakatoa Comes to Life

Up until the early part of 1883, Krakatoa was considered a dead volcano. It had not erupted ash or lava flows as long as anyone could remember. The islanders told stories of Krakatoa's violent eruptions long ago. They also said that the spirit of the volcano god, Orang Alijeh, would breathe fire and smoke when things were not going well.

BER 29, 1883.   HARPER'S WEEKLY.

THE ISLAND AND VOLCANO OF KRAKATOA, STRAIT OF SUNDA, SUBMERGED DURING THE LATE ERUPTION.—[See Page 614.]

Krakatoa was a stratovolcano. Most people thought that it was dead, meaning that it no longer erupted. This drawing of Krakatoa appeared in the September 29, 1883 edition of *Harper's Weekly*.

They even warned that the volcano spirit was angry at the way the Dutch were treating the islanders. (The Dutch had colonized a portion of the East Indies to take advantage of the profitable spice trade with Southeast Asia.) But for the Europeans who lived there and the many ships that passed through the busy Sundra Strait, the island was simply an extinct volcano.

On May 10, 1883, the lighthouse keeper on Java noticed that the rumbling was a little different from the usual activity. He noted it in his logbooks. About five days later, stronger and longer rumblings motivated a Dutch official from Sumatra to inform his superiors that something unusual was happening.

The first visible event was more surprising than dangerous. At 10:30 A.M. on May 20, Captain Hollmann of the German warship *Elisabeth* reported seeing "a white cumulus cloud, rising fast."[1] The ship's chaplain noted that by the next morning everything on the ship was covered with a gray, sticky dust. Other ships in the area reported lightning flashes deep within the clouds billowing from the volcano. The ships' compass needles spun around wildly.

Summer came. At first, life went on as usual, even as Krakatoa became more active. Its three volcanic craters were coming to life one by one. The May 20 eruption came from the northernmost crater known as Perboewatan.

This eruption followed by the eruption of Danan, the middle crater, on June 16. By August 10, the third and largest crater, Rakata, began to release steam and pieces of lava. The pieces of lava cooled in the air, forming a lightweight volcanic rock called pumice. Day and night, the air that summer was filled with the sounds of the volcano. The eruptions sounded like rifle shots and cannon fire. Yet these explosions were mild compared to the sights and sounds on the afternoon of August 26.

The Sun Disappears

In Anjer, Java, Mr. Schruit, the telegraph master, heard an explosion a great deal louder than any before. He turned toward Krakatoa and saw clouds of ash rising from the mountain "as if thousands of white balloons had been released from the crater."[2] Some claimed to see black clouds; others saw the colors alternate. Ash blotted out the sunlight. Within minutes, Anjer was cloaked in an artificial night. The official time of the eruption was marked as 1:06 P.M. local time.

As evening approached, Krakatoa erupted with even greater force. Explosions sounded more and more often. About this time, the sea became more violent. Waves rushed inland then receded far back from the shore, making it seem as if the sea had disappeared.

Krakatoa exploded, sending giant ocean waves toward the nearby islands. In this drawing, lightning can be seen above the eruption.

The Tsunamis Hit

On August 27, Krakatoa's explosions became less frequent but more explosive. Its last four explosions at 5:30 A.M., 6:44 A.M., 8:20 A.M., and 10:02 A.M. generated the tsunamis that did the most damage. By 6:00 A.M., Ketimbang on Sumatra was completely destroyed. A few minutes later, Anjer on Java was wiped away leaving only a few survivors. R. A. van Sandick, an engineer aboard the steamer *Loudon*, watched as a tsunami hit the town of Telok Betong between 7:30 and 8:30 A.M.:

> The light tower could be seen to tumble; the houses disappeared; the steamer *Berouw* was lifted and got stuck, apparently at the height of the cocoanut trees; and everything had become sea in front of our eyes, . . . The impressiveness of this scene is difficult to describe. . . . The best comparison is a sudden change of scenery, which in a fairy tale occurs by a fairy's magic wand, but on a colossal scale and with the conscious knowledge that it is reality and that thousands of people have perished in an indivisible moment, that destruction without equal has been wrought.[3]

The volcano finally exploded at 10:02 A.M., leaving only a small portion of what was once the 2,600-foot mountain of Krakatoa. Most of the island that Krakatoa was on was destroyed. The last explosion sent out ocean waves, sound waves, and shock waves. The local tsunamis were as high as 130 feet. The eruption also generated ocean waves that registered on tide gauges as far away as Europe. The sound waves were heard over three thousand miles away, and the shock wave traveled around the world seven times.

Today, within the crater of the old Krakatoa is a new volcano, Anak Krakatoa. Its name means "child of Krakatoa." Tourists can take boat trips to the new island to see the volcano up close. To the locals, the active Anak Krakatoa is a good reminder of the potentially violent explosions that can occur at any time.

Little remains of the damage from Krakatoa in 1883. However, whole towns that were buried by the A.D. 79 eruption of Mount Vesuvius have been discovered.

Fumaroles can be seen on the side of Anak Krakatoa. When magma travels through a small crack and comes into contact with ground water, fumaroles often form. This produces steam which comes out the side of the mountain.

CHAPTER 4

Vesuvius: History Frozen in Time

MOUNT VESUVIUS ERUPTED ON AUGUST 24, IN the year A.D. 79. Death came suddenly to the people of Pompeii and Herculaneum as they went about their daily activities. At that time, no one understood volcanoes or knew what to expect during an eruption. Many simply waited and watched. As the eruption continued, ash and volcanic debris covered the area. The towns of Pompeii and Herculaneum stayed buried for more than fourteen hundred years.

The first artifacts from Pompeii were discovered in the late 1500s. However, it was not until much later, in 1763, that people realized that they had indeed found the lost city. As Pompeii was uncovered, many details of the daily life of a Roman city were revealed. It was lunchtime at the time of the eruption. The priests were having eggs

Today, Pompeii looks very much as it did before it was buried over two thousand years ago.

and fish. One family left a pig roasting in the oven and another left meat in its cooking pot. Other people were found trying to flee with their jewels and other treasures. There were even two prisoners found in the jail at the gladiator's barracks.

In 1861, Guiseppe Fiorelli, the professor of archaeology in charge of the ruins, made a great discovery. He realized that as the bodies of the victims deteriorated within the hardened volcanic material, they left spaces that could be filled with liquid plaster. When the plaster hardened and the volcanic material was chipped away, there remained an exact replica of the person's body, clothes, and even facial expressions.

Plaster molds of victims of Vesuvius show how the people looked when they were killed by the powerful volcano.

The resulting casts of positions and faces tell a tale of extreme agony. Families were found together, parents trying to protect their young children. A father and daughter lay in their garden, the daughter's face buried in her father's clothes as she tries to breathe. A mule driver found by the gymnasium wall crouches down, covering his face to avoid breathing the fumes.

The Death of Pliny the Elder

One eyewitness was a teenager known as Pliny the Younger. He wrote two letters to his friend, the historian Tacitus, telling him what happened that day. The first letter tells his uncle's story. His uncle, Pliny the Elder, was an admiral of a Roman fleet at Misenum. He was also a naturalist who collected many facts about animals and plants.

He had written thirty-seven volumes titled *Natural History*. In his honor, highly explosive eruptions like the one at Vesuvius are named Plinian eruptions.

As Pliny the Elder observed the strange cloud above the distant mountains, he determined to get a closer look. As he prepared to take his boat out, he received a note from a friend's wife, Rectina. She asked him to come to her villa at the foot of Vesuvius and rescue her. He wanted to rescue not only Rectina, but also many others who lived in the area. "He hurried to a place from which

Vesuvius destroyed many of the surrounding towns when it erupted. Some towns were completely covered with lava.

others were fleeing, and held his course directly into danger . . . he kept up a continuous observation of the various movements and shapes of that evil cloud, dictating what he saw."[1] As his boat neared the area of the volcano, the shore was blocked with pumice stones. The extent of the destruction soon became clearer. At the urging of his helmsman, he turned to Stabiae, home of his friend Pomponianus.

Pliny the Elder managed to dock at Stabiae. With panic all around him, he tried to calm others by carrying on as if nothing unusual was happening. His nephew wrote, "He bathed and dined, carefree or at least appearing so. . . . Meanwhile, broad sheets of flame were lighting up many parts of Vesuvius; their light and brightness were the more vivid for the darkness of the night."[2] While getting some rest, the volcanic ash began to pile up around his door and his companions urged him to leave. As he was walking to the boat, he was overcome by the heated air and died in the street.

Pliny the Younger Perseveres

Meanwhile, Pliny the Younger and his mother stayed at home in Misenum. They stayed outdoors through the night as the ground tremors threatened the buildings around them. In the morning, they decided to leave. Pliny the Younger noted that the carts they used would not stay put, even with stones blocking the wheels. "Then we saw the sea sucked back . . . and many sea creatures were left stranded on the dry sand. . . . From the other direction, over the land, a dreadful black cloud was torn by gushing, twisting, flames [glowing, red-hot ash], and great tongues of fire like much-magnified lightning . . ."[3]

Pliny and his mother found themselves alternately at a standstill or pushed forward in the crush of people leaving the city. They decided to get off the main road and wait

Vesuvius is still active today.

for a while. ". . . darkness fell upon us. . . . We could hear women shrieking, children crying, and men shouting."[4] The pair waited out the darkness. When the sky light-ened, it was only for a short while. "The darkness came back and ash began to fall again, this time in heavier showers. We had to get up from time to time to shake it off or we would have been crushed and buried under its weight."[5] Finally, daylight returned and they went back home.

> ". . . a dreadful black cloud was torn by gushing, twisting, flames, and great tongues of fire . . ."
>
> —Pliny the Younger

Pompeii is still of interest today and excavation continues there and in nearby Herculaneum. In 2000, archaeologists uncovered another forty-eight victims in Herculaneum. The archaeologists still take casts of what they find, but now they inject the cavities with silicone rubber instead of liquid plaster.

The residents near Mount St. Helens were not as sur-prised as those of Pompeii and Herculaneum. However, Mount St. Helens would be an eruption that drew the attention of the world.

The Story of Mount St. Helens

MOUNT ST. HELENS WAS ONE OF THE BEST documented eruptions. It demonstrated many of the events that can occur during a volcanic eruption.

The eruption began on March 20, 1980, when a 4.2 magnitude earthquake was recorded directly under Mount St. Helens. Magnitude, measured on a scale of 0 to 10, records the earth's vibrations. A 2.5 to 3.0 magnitude quake can be felt, and a 5.0 quake will break windows and shake items off of shelves.

This initial earthquake was not large. However, a week later, a small crater opened up on the summit. Steam and hot ash shot from the crater into the air almost daily. By the beginning of May, the mile-high displays of ash and steam stopped. Seismometers continued to show activity under the surface of Mount St. Helens.

Mount St. Helens lost over one thousand feet in elevation from the 1980 eruption.

Meanwhile, a portion of the north side of the mountain began to bulge outward. Soon after, the May 18 blast occurred.

Sound Waves Play Tricks

No one within about sixty miles of the crater heard the blast. Sound travels faster in warm air than in cool air. The cooler air near the top of the volcano, traveling slower, pulled the sound waves up. This created a "shadow zone" that the sound could not reach. Robert Barrett was fishing on Silver Lake that morning with his wife. He later reported, "Suddenly an eerie quiet surrounded us. No insect noise, no birds chirped, the fish completely stopped biting, my watch stopped and the sky began to darken. We looked at one another and said in unison 'Oh my God the mountain.'"[1]

While those closest to the volcano heard nothing, people far away definitely heard the blast. Dan A. Nelson was picking mushrooms in the Blue Mountains of Southeast Washington, several hundred miles away. "The 'boom' echoed through the air. For the next 15 minutes, the air rattled with a sound like 100 planes going supersonic in the middle of a thunderstorm. We all knew instantly what it was."[2]

Ash and Mudslides Wreak Havoc

In addition to the sideways blast, a huge plume of steam, ash, and rock shot up over twelve miles into the air. A man living about thirty miles away noted, "My wife and I went out the front door and saw . . . a magnificent sight. It was like an atom bomb going off on the top of St. Helens."[3] Tons of ash spread eastward over twenty-two thousand square miles in the first nine hours of the eruption.

When the mountain released its hot material, about 70 percent of its snow and ice melted instantly. This hot

This car was buried in one of Mount St. Helens' mudslides.

water, combined with ash and other debris, created a warm mudslide. It sped down the mountain at eighty miles per hour. Most of the mudflow joined the Toutle River. Along the north fork of the river, mud and debris wiped out houses, bridges, and roads.

Events Surprise Onlookers

The onset of volcanic activity earlier in March had brought many curious people to Mount St. Helens. Not all of them lived to tell about the eruption. Many of the dead were found with cameras still in their hands. However, the eruption's circumstances saved untold numbers of lives. First, the eruption happened on a Sunday morning before over three hundred loggers began working on the mountain. Second, the eruption blew to the sparsely populated northwest rather than toward the area around the city of Portland. Third, the forewarning of volcanic activity gave officials time to evacuate the area.

Some who stayed behind, such as David Johnston, accepted the risks involved. Others, like Buzz Smith, were not always aware of the risks. He and his sons had been camping in the area. They had to walk fifteen miles through the ash storm before they were found and evacuated. "We're a logging community," said Buzz Smith. "I don't think anyone in this area really had any idea of the destruction that the mountain could cause . . . nothing

The huge eruption left this gaping crater at the top of Mount St. Helens.

like what happened. I never in my wildest dreams could have imagined it."[4]

In 2004, Mount St. Helens started to have small eruptions, and the lava dome inside its crater began to grow. Time will only tell whether the volcano will have another major eruption.

Scientists continue to learn more about volcanoes. They help predict eruptions, protect people, and even point out how volcanoes benefit both man and nature.

6

Hazards and Benefits

STUDYING THE ERUPTIONS OF VOLCANOES HIGH-lights the hazards. There is also a positive, helpful side to eruptions. Volcanic ash covers the ground and becomes a fertile soil, excellent for farming. Volcanic ash and lava are both useful for making household products.

Lava

Lava moves slowly and people usually have time to flee from danger. Very few people are killed by lava. The main threats are to property and agriculture because lava surrounds, covers, or ignites anything in its path. Even though lava destroys, it also creates. When lava flows out into the sea, it cools into rock. The cooled lava piles up until it is above the surface, creating new land. Hawaii's Kilauea volcano has created 540 acres of new land in the last twenty years.

Lava does not always flow gently from a vent. When lava is full of gas bubbles, it can be thrown from a volcano explosively. As the lava cools in the air, the gas is expelled, leaving holes that make a very light rock called pumice. It is the only rock that floats on water.

Man has found many uses for pumice. It is used to remove dead skin, especially from the feet. In the United States, pumice is also used by clothing manufacturers to make stonewashed jeans.

Volcanic Ash

Volcanic ash has become a valuable natural resource. Today, volcanic ash is made into clay, called bentonite. Bentonite is used as a filler in adhesives and ceramics. Because it absorbs moisture, bentonite is a major ingredient in kitty litter. Fine-grained ash is used as a polishing agent in toothpaste and household cleaners.

Living Near a Volcano

Some people choose to live near volcanoes for the fertile soil, others for the beauty and excitement. One man who lives on Mount Etna in Italy expresses it this way: "Etna is like a mother to us, she feeds us and protects us, even though she [sometimes acts] like a cruel stepmother."[1] Although Donna and Steve O'Meara met in Boston, Massachusetts, their second date was a helicopter trip

Volcanoes often blanket nearby towns with ash.

over a volcano in Kilauea, Hawaii. A year later, they were married beside a lava flow. After many return trips, they decided to move there. They have lived on the volcano for over ten years. Donna O'Meara said, "Living here, we see nature's beauty and ferocity up close. I feel really privileged to have a front row seat."[2]

Warning Systems

The Volcano Disaster Assistance Program of the United States provides rapid response to areas threatened by

Volcanoes can be very beautiful, but people should be careful when visiting them. Usually scientists will issue a warning for people to stay clear of a volcano. These tourists flee as a volcano in Mexico erupts.

a volcano. Volcano experts are dispatched to crisis areas to work with local scientists and officials. They set up portable monitoring equipment to give local officials timely information on the volcano's activity. This helps them decide when to put their disaster plans into action. Just before Pinatubo erupted in the Philippines in 1991, officials at nearby Clark Air Base evacuated 14,500 American servicemen and their families. Captain Randal L. Carr recalls, "It's hard to describe the ordeal that transpired at the hands of Pinatubo. I can recall a sense of teamwork that outweighed the tremendous odds we faced."[3]

Volcano Safety

A good disaster plan starts with a hazard map that shows what to expect from a volcano. This map is based on the volcano's past and present activity. The map should include information on potential ash clouds, lava bomb areas, noxious gases, and tsunamis. It should also show the potential or most likely direction of lava flows, mudflows, pyroclastic flows, and debris avalanches.

A disaster plan also includes monitoring stations, a warning system, and an evacuation plan. Local communities are then educated to help them prepare for all scenarios. They need to

People who lived near Pinatubo had to be well prepared when the volcano erupted.

Masks are good protection from volcanic ash.

know how and where to evacuate. If they remain in the area during the eruption, they need to have a disaster supply kit. People can protect themselves from one of the biggest hazards, volcanic ash. The ash is made up of very fine, glassy fragments that can cause severe damage to breathing passages, eyes, and open wounds. The kit should include goggles and disposable breathing masks to help protect a person from the ash.

Much progress has been made in the last fifty years in monitoring volcanoes. As more is learned, more accurate predictions can be made. However, like other forces of nature, volcanoes require preparation before disaster strikes. It is the best way to save lives.

World's Deadliest Volcanoes

Place	Date	Deaths
Tambora, Indonesia	1815	92,000
Krakatoa, Indonesia	1883	36,417
Mount Pelée, Martinique	1902	29,025
Ruiz, Colombia	1985	25,000
Unzen, Japan	1792	14,300
Laki, Iceland	1783	9,350
Kelut, Indonesia	1919	5,110
Galunggung, Indonesia	1882	4,011
Vesuvius, Italy	1631	3,500
Vesuvius, Italy	79	3,360
Papandayan, Indonesia	1772	2,957

Chapter Notes

Chapter 1. Mount St. Helens Blows Its Top

1. Jelle Zeilinga de Boer and Donald Theodore Sanders, *Volcanoes in Human History: The Far-Reaching Effects of Major Eruptions* (Princeton, N.J.: Princeton University Press, 2002), p. 236.

2. "Debris Avalanche," *U.S. Geological Survey*, March 19, 2002, <http://pubs.usgs.gov/publications/msh/debris.html> (July 3, 2004).

3. "On This Day," *BBC*, 2004, <http://news.bbc.co.uk/ onthisday/hi/dates/stories/may/19/newsid_2511000/ 2511133.stm> (September 27, 2004).

Chapter 2. Volcanoes Up Close

1. Alwyn Scarth, *Vulcan's Fury: Man Against the Volcano* (New Haven, Conn.: Yale University Press, 1999), p. 197.

2. Simon Winchester, *Krakatoa* (New York: Harper Collins Publishers, 2003), p. 161.

Chapter 3. Krakatoa Makes Waves

1. Simon Winchester, *Krakatoa* (New York: Harper Collins Publishers, 2003), p. 157.

2. Ibid., p. 212.

3. Ibid., pp. 249–250.

Chapter 4. Vesuvius: History Frozen in Time

1. Cynthia Damon, *Pliny Letter 6.16.*, n.d. <http:// www.amherst.edu/~classics/class36/ancsrc/01.html> (July 3, 2004).

2. Ibid.

3. Alwyn Scarth, *Vulcan's Fury* (New Haven, Conn.: Yale University Press, 1999), p. 35.

4. Ibid., p. 35.

5. Ibid., p. 36.

Chapter 5. The Story of Mount St. Helens

1. Robert Barrett, *Letter 3: Bass tournament stopped by volcano*, n.d., <http://www.thesunlink.com/packages/helens/letter3.html> (July 3, 2004).

2. Dan A. Nelson, Special to *The Seattle Times, Lifestyles*: Thursday, May 25, 2000, <http://seattletimes.nwsource.com/helens/story5.html> (July 3, 2004).

3. Randall Lovett, "Mount St. Helens: From the Ashes," *Seattle Post-Intelligencer*, n.d., <http://seattlepi.nwsource.com/mountsthelens/mem2.shtml> (July 3, 2004).

4. Cynthia Gorney, "A Stifling Darkness Descended," *The Washington Post*, May 25, 1980, p. A1.

Chapter 6. Hazards and Benefits

1. Alwyn Scarth, *Vulcan's Fury* (New Haven, Conn.: Yale University Press, 1999), p. 58.

2. Brian Handwerk for *National Geographic News*, "Hawaii's Kilauea Lava Flow: 20 Years and Counting," January 3, 2003, <http://news.nationalgeographic.com/news/2003/01/0102_030103_kilauea.html> (July 3, 2004).

3. Captain Randal L. Carr, *Journal, Clark Air Base: VOLCON 5*, n.d., <http://randalcarr.tripod.com/pinatubo/journal.htm> (July 3, 2004).

Glossary

ductile—Able to be molded into another shape or form. The earth's mantle is ductile.

lava—The name for molten rock, or magma, after it escapes a volcano's vent.

magma—Molten rock inside the earth's crust.

magnitude—A measurement of vibrations in the earth using a logarithmic scale.

mantle—The layer of earth between the crust and the core.

mudflow—A mixture of water and other debris created as snow or ice melts. The heat from a volcano melts snow and ice, creating a warm mixture that moves quickly.

plates—Large, relatively rigid pieces of the earth's crust. Plates fit together like a jigsaw puzzle. Volcanic activity takes place mostly along the edges of plates.

pumice—Lightweight volcanic rock created as gas-filled lava cools. The gas leaves numerous holes throughout the rock, making it light enough to float on water.

pyroclastic flows—Spinning mixtures of very hot gases and pieces of volcanic rocks in various sizes. These flows shoot down the side of the volcano at very high speeds.

seismometers—Devices that measure movement or vibrations of the earth's crust.

shock waves—Pressure waves that travel through the air.

summit—The highest point, or peak, of a mountain or volcano.

tsunami—A large ocean wave created by a volcano or other subterranean movement.

vent—An opening in a volcano where gas, steam, or lava can escape.

Further Reading

Books

Challen, Paul. *Volcano Alert!* New York: Crabtree Publishing, 2004.

Furgang, Kathy. *Krakatoa: History's Loudest Volcano*. New York: PowerKids Press, 2001.

———. *Mount Vesuvius: Europe's Mighty Volcano of Smoke and Ash*. New York: PowerKids Press, 2001.

Leigh, Autumn. *Warning: Volcano!: The Story of Mount St. Helens*. New York: Rosen, 2002.

Montardre, Hâeláene. *Volcanoes: Journey to the Crater's Edge*, adapted by Robert Burleigh. New York: H. N. Abrams, 2003.

Rice, Melanie and Christopher. *Pompeii: The Day a City Was Buried*. New York: DK Publishing, 1998.

Spilsbury, Richard and Louise. *Violent Volcanoes*. Oxford: Heinemann Library, 2004.

Trueit, Trudi Strain. *Volcanoes*. New York: Franklin Watts, 2003.

Webster, Christine. *Mauna Loa: The Largest Volcano in the United States*. New York: Weigl Publishers, Inc., 2004.

Internet Addresses

Smithsonian Institution—Global Volcanism Program
<http://www.volcano.si.edu>

U.S. Geological Survey Volcano Hazards Program
<http://volcanoes.usgs.gov>

Volcano World
<http://volcano.und.nodak.edu>

Index